THE PATH

THE WAY TO NEW BEGINNING

EBY ALEX

Copyright © Eby Alex
All Rights Reserved.

This book has been published with all efforts taken to make the material error-free after the consent of the author. However, the author and the publisher do not assume and hereby disclaim any liability to any party for any loss, damage, or disruption caused by errors or omissions, whether such errors or omissions result from negligence, accident, or any other cause.

While every effort has been made to avoid any mistake or omission, this publication is being sold on the condition and understanding that neither the author nor the publishers or printers would be liable in any manner to any person by reason of any mistake or omission in this publication or for any action taken or omitted to be taken or advice rendered or accepted on the basis of this work. For any defect in printing or binding the publishers will be liable only to replace the defective copy by another copy of this work then available.

I dedicate this book to my wife & family, they have been absolute support to me in all my life.

Contents

Preface

I'm so happy to present a gift to all of you, it is nothing but this book, I am thankful to each one of you from the bottom of my heart for considering my little work in your collection. I praise God for being my mysterious guide throughout my life. Furthermore, I have seen so many people working so hard and myself read so many books that show how to develop ourselves as a person, all those experiences and knowledge led me into this. As Einstein said, **"There comes a point in your life when you need to stop reading other people's books and write your own."** I have been inspired by people who have done things that they like to do from the beginning till the end. All those gains triggered me to think about the people who are working so hard and still there is nothing great happening. I started thinking about what they are missing, then an Idea came to my mind, a thought, in this book from chapter one to end I tried my level best to explain it. It is interesting though, we all know the journey of life is difficult and there is no other choice we should travel one way or the other, but if you have a goal, or you know something you want, you should first move to a certain point to travel the path and achieve the goal. This book largely focuses on how to move from the current position to the exact starting point. For example, if you wanted to go to a certain place via bus, first we need to go to the bus stop, in order to go to the bus stop we can choose a different path, this book will help you find the exact path to reach the bus stop and get into the right bus. How that bus will travel I don't know, but this book will make sure you are boarding the right bus.

Acknowledgements

I'm extremely grateful to the almighty that leads and guides me in each and every second of my life. I would like to express my sincere thanks to my dearest teachers and mentors who have taught me in the right way. Furthermore, I am thankful that God has given me a life and freedom to think, otherwise this book will not be possible. I cannot forget the MS Office and tools also other online offline writing tools without it, all this will be very difficult. A special thanks to sweetheart, for the push that I required when I'm down. Last but not least, I would like to express my deepest thanks to notion press for providing me not only a platform but also the right tools to publish this dream book. This book is one of my many dreams, thanks to all who helped me to become what I'm today.

Prologue

We all have dreams and goals that we wanted to achieve, sometimes we win, sometimes we lose. But whatever the situation, are you sure you are moving towards the right path? Are you sure your choices are the best one? This book aims to make sure that the path followed by you is the correct one. This book is like a friend who guides you or gives you the right perceptions. It covers a variety of topics that will help you in most of the situation you will come across in your life. Even though the content is experimental, I can assure a better change in your mindset will happen once you finish reading this book. Last but not least, I thank you for choosing my book, My prayers will be with you even though I'm not known to you.

ONE
THE PATH

The path is all about life, most of the scenarios mentioned here are based on my personal experiences and the experiences that I learned from my friends and colleagues. Before going into the book, I want to ask you a question. What do you mean by a path to you? I know you got a picture in your head right now. It may be a picture of a street or maybe a pathway to your house or a big road in your favorite video game or the most common image of Robert Frost's "Road not taken." Anyway, a lot of pictures, ideas, and thoughts came into our minds. But my dear friends, did you get a picture of you traveling on the path toward your dreams?

If yes, then the book is not for you. You do not require this book. You are in a better position in terms of mindset. Maybe better than me. But if you are not getting the picture of you, my dear friend, you must read this book no matter what situation you are in and thank me later. I promise you will not regret your life.

How to read this book?

I know all of you knew how to read a book, but if you are reading this book, I would suggest you follow some suggestions given below:

- Read daily at least fifteen minutes, if completed, re-read.
- Make mandatory notes and form your structure based on the data given in the book.
- Do the exercises which are mentioned in the book if it is required.
- Do not judge the content of the book, if you like it follow it, and make use of it.
- Once you understand the core of this book, if you felt it is useful, share it with your friends and colleagues.

This could be the best way to read this book, in fact, this would be the best way to read any book. In case you have any suggestions, issues, or assistance required, please feel to chat with me as well.

What is a path?

Definition of the path given by google; "way or track laid down for walking or made by continual treading." Simply path means a route to reach somewhere, right? Yes, it is. Let's take a scenario where you want to go to the point; B from the point; A, you knew the starting point and the destination. But your time required for travel, speed of travel, type of travel, mode of travel, the distance of travel and, so many other things are decided by the path you choose to travel. That is why the path is much more important than the goal you are aiming for. Every decision in your life revolves around the path you decide.

Most people do not give much importance to the path, because nobody talks about how they achieved success or their particular dream. People only talk about, how were they? And how they do right now. There is a large amount of data and experience that is untold, it is not because they want to keep it a secret, it is because nobody wants to hear. Here I tried to figure out a method to abstract the untold story and use it for our own life success. Here, the definition of the path is the route to which we travel to success. Our path is simple and much useful, even you may pass it to the next generation as well. You may use this path irrespective of your financial status, color, race religion, and type of dream you wanted to achieve.

To be honest, your starting point has no significance in your destination, so do not worry about the situation that you are in right now. The most important thing you should understand is the path you choose is the fate of your life.

The first thing we are going to look at is, are you on the right path? Do you need a path? Keep reading, it won't disappoint you.

Why path is required?

The path is required because it is your fate! Yes, it is. No matter how much you crib cry about free will and stuff, fate is always there but, there is one thing, the fate of your life destined by nothing but the path you decide. If you are well aware of your path, then all the expectations and predictions about your life will be kosher by this time. The reality in most cases is not true. This is the most indispensable reason for selecting the right path wisely. There are a few other reasons as well. The path is required to show your identity because identity is something that defines us. The path is required to travel the journey of life because without knowing a way to travel you will be unable to move forward. You will become stagnant and depressed, and that is not good. I hope you don't want to be like that. The salient thing you should consider if you do not have a proper path, is how you are going to take care of your next generation? That is one hell of a question you should ask yourself. If you have a good path with all the necessary support, then the best thing you could pass on to the next generation is the knowledge about how to build their path. So, simply put, the choice of the best path will eventually lead to a prodigious life that you always dreamed of.

Am I on the right path?

Ask yourself this question, how do you feel? I know it's hard to say. Most people have the same problem, but you could check whether you are on the right path or not. There are a few steps given below. Following these steps, you will be able to see whether you are in the right direction or not.

- Take a personality test and verify its result. Check whether the result is matching with the current you or not.
- Take a deep breath to relax and analyze your memory, if more positive thoughts, appearing then you are on the right path.
- Write down your achievements and check whether those achievements, help to your ultimate goal.
- Did you feel bored in your work or excited?
- Are you always feeling sad or excited?
- If you think all these are nonsense and just jokes, then definitely you are on the wrong path.

So, answer these questions and analyze yourself to find out your current direction.

How do get on to the right path?

The entire book is concentrated on two things, 75 percent of the book looks forward to teaching you about how to get into the correct path, the rest 25 percent focuses on how to stay on the correct path to achieve dreams and goals.

If you are aware, there are so many books, videos, social media content that will motivate you to stay on the right path but what I would try to do is to inspire you to reach the right path first then travel throughout life and achieve your dreams and goals.

From here the real journey starts, be ready for the fun, guys. In this session, I'm assuming you have a goal or a dream to reach and an open mindset. If not also no problem, in the coming chapters we will be learning, how to get a goal and an open mindset. Well, without wasting much time, let's take an example, consider your goal is to open your restaurant, right now you are a hard earning employee with a beautiful wife and kid, for your information, it is just an example. Now you are aware that by opening a good restaurant you will be able to balance your finances and enjoy the life you always wanted to be. You tried several ways to open one, but all attempts failed, you planned such as which date to open, about investments, about expenses, about location, about everything that you know but still, you are unable to open. What went wrong? How did he fail? Despite having an open mindset and a good amount of knowledge, why does he keep failing?

There could be numerous reasons, but there is some unavoidable reason.

- The first thing is fixing the target, here the man was about to start a restaurant well, the target is financial freedom, so the question you may have is a restaurant business is a right choice?
- It could be the right choice if he designed the plan according to the ultimate goal. So, the plan may not be as good as he expected
- One of the most important reasons might be he is only focusing on the monetary value.

These are a few reasons that one should avoid in the process of building something. In this book, I tried my best to figure out a solution for this. But before we begin, I would love to give few tips.

- Consider you already started the restaurant business, start thinking backward so in the reverse order you will be able to reach the first step, remember this first step is the step towards your goal. In this book, I mainly focus on how to reach the first step? Which is your initial path.
- When you think backward, you know that you will reach an initial point. Compare your current state of life with it. You will get an idea of how far you are from it. I will help you to fill up that gap also travel further ahead in your life.
- Be ready to do the activities and functions mentioned in this book and use them to achieve success in your life.

TWO
FIRST STEP

Here in this chapter, we will be moving towards the steps to initiate the changes required to make our path to reach the initial stage of the goal.

1. *Share your goal with your close ones:*

The first step is to close, one is for you to interact, not them to respond every time. Share your goal with your close ones, you must tell them what exactly you want? What did you want to do? Every possible detail. Discuss with them because you will need mental support from them when no one is around. Keep in mind that they don't have to understand everything you say. You should be open to them. The close one can be your mother, father, siblings, girlfriend, anyone who is close to you. The point of having a close one is for you to interact, not for them to respond every time.

2. *Grouping Pros & Cons.*

Now, the second important step is grouping the pros and cons. First, how you should do it? The answer, sit with your close one then takes a paper, write down the pros and cons. It doesn't matter if it is in proper order or not. All you have to do is to list them separately. While writing pros and cons it should include pros for you, your family, close one, friends, and finally mankind. Now if the number of pros is higher than the cons then you can go ahead with your plan or goal. If the cons are higher than the pros, then your goal needs to be modified. Modification of a goal doesn't mean you change it, it means the approach of the goal and its expectations, need to be changed.

3. Modification of goal.

This step is only needed if modification is required. If your cons are higher, then modification is required. The catch here is either you can change your ultimate goal or you may eradicate the cons to balance the present goal. I will suggest you reduce the cons to modify your goal.

Now the question is how to eradicate it? Well, that is easy. First, write down the cons separately, in the second column write down why these cons are happening.

Now in the third column, write down what will be the after-effects of these cons. In the fourth column, write is possible to avoid these cons if it is possible to mention yes if not no. Now let's take out the cons that you mentioned, yes. Consider these small cons as a miniature goal inside your ultimate goal. Now, again, repeat the steps we followed initially. Takedown pros and cons for your miniature goal, sort it out, take out solvable cons, consider them as miniature goals, again repeat the steps. It may sound messy and complex, but trust me, this is way easier and more effective when you put it into action. Sometimes you will be fascinated that the entire cons will go away in just a matter of time.

Now in case of the cons that you mentioned not, those cons which you felt unsolvable, note it down separately. Check once more is unsolvable. If yes, then check, it is necessary to eliminate these cons. If not, then leave it. If yes, you have to go to your ultimate goal since we have the steps in backward to check which step poses the trouble here, make changes to that particular step so that you will be able to eliminate the unsolvable cons.

You might have a few doubts about changing the steps in the goal, then we could have done it for every con, that would be easy, right. Yes, it is easy but, your entire goal will change so, the path will change then there is no use in all this hard work. Therefore, you must proceed with the steps mentioned above. These might be time-consuming but, it is worth a shot. You may take help from the chosen one during the sorting process, which will change goal to goal and person to person.

4. Execution of process

In this step, we will start executing our steps. According to the sorting and detailing done in the previous step. Remember, execution required a lot of knowledge and a strong mindset. Initial execution of steps won't help you to achieve the goals. But it will help you to reach the initial step towards your ultimate goal from your present state. Which means it will help you find your path.

THREE
THE ESSENTIALS

Well, we know our goal. We know how to get rid of the problems, cons, and almost every negativity. The important part left is to execute the idea. So far, whatever we did was on paper, we have to practically apply it. To do that, what we required most is the mindset. So far, we assumed we have an open, ideal, mindset but in reality, that is not the case. Some people don't even understand what it is all about, open mindset and stuff, people are talking a lot about it. So, our first thing here is to open up our mindset. It is essential, like how oxygen is for our life.

How to open our mindset?

To open our mindset, we should understand how the brain works. Our brain works based on conditioning. What is conditioning? Conditioning is the process by which something is getting molded into a particular shape over some time. For example, in small classes, we learned that the sun rises on the east and sets in the west. Technically, it is not right, but our brain adapted the information and accepted it as valid. That means your brain will accept data if you are providing it consistently, which doesn't matter right or wrong. Your brain will accept the provided command or data. Here when I say brain, I mean the subconscious part of the brain. So, the first thing is to condition your brain according to your goal. Keep in mind that, you like the process of conditioning the brain or not by the course of continuous conditioning, the subconscious will adapt and respond accordingly. Here you might encounter a problem such as you may feel it hard to recondition your brain, so what you have to do is to take help from the closest people that we chose to be part of your journey at the beginning. How can they help you with this situation? They have to push you, push your limits to get adapted to new conditioning. Changing conditioning and its effect will vary from person to person. Sometimes it might be a new addition to the existing habits or an entirely new habit. To change conditioning, you may have to talk to the people you did not want to talk to, may have to do stuff that you were not imagined doing in your life, etc. The person helping you must take responsibility to help you change your conditioning in case you required help.

Now another important thing that is required to open mind is nonjudgmental behavior. That is one hell of a behavior that most people fail to have. Because we all will judge in some part of our life, but I am telling you if you want to change and figure out your correct path, please don't be judgmental. You already don't know which path to choose to reach the initial point of your goal because of judgments and, our judgment is always relative. For example, killing a person is wrong. Everybody knows that it cannot be applied on the battlefield. On a battlefield, we must fight against the enemy, and we should come victorious otherwise, what will happen the enemy will defeat us and maybe kill us. The thing you should understand here is this process can take time depending upon your urge, desire, etc. the more you are driven by a desire for your goal, you'll get attached to the process and you'll follow the process to achieve your goals. So, once you have the nonjudgmental character and right conditioning, you will have an open mindset also. Having an open mindset is unavoidable because this open mindset and nonjudgmental character is the basis of your execution of the steps to reach the initial point of your goal. Simply, say the requirements to start the change.

Once you have an open mindset and have enough control over it, the next important step is to control your emotions. Without controlling emotions at the right time, you cannot achieve the success you want controlling, in the sense, it doesn't mean that you should not show your emotions. It means you have to show the right emotions at the right time and not show them when it is not the right time. The funniest catch here is controlling your emotions should come from your inside, which means you cannot just stop talking to people or not showing to the public, or not talking to a crowd or your friend. That is not controlling emotions that are running away from emotion. Since you have an open mindset, it is just a matter of time before you will acquire the ability to control your emotions. In the subsequent chapters, we will be discussing how to control emotions.

How to control emotions?

Controlling emotions are not that difficult as you thought there are few ways to control it as its best first, we should understand how many types of emotions we have there are two types of emotions a person possesses the first one is real emotion and the second one is imaginary emotion or unreal emotion. you may wonder how emotions can be imaginary or unreal, but the truth is it is there it can be. There are only two emotions that are real in the world, is love and pain except two, all other emotions that we possess are imaginary or, you can say personal illusions. Trust me, love and pain are the emotion that has the power to control your life rest of the emotions such as hate, anger, anxiety, extra, did not have power over your life but, we often submit ourselves under the control of these imaginary or personal illusionist emotions.

let's take an example, say you hated a person very much but, a long time ago you loved that same person a lot that time you hugged, kissed, exchanged gifts, help each other, took care of each other. Now you hate each other so much that you might kill that person. The question is, how can you show your hate towards that person? You may keep your mouth shut, you may not talk to that person, you can show anger to that person, you can even kill that person. But if you hate that person, how many times have you killed a person? How many times did you show anger? You can kill that person only once, it doesn't matter, you showing anger the first time or the hundredth time the anger remains the same, the effect remains the same, he already knew that you hate him. so, what is the point of showing it over and over again? He already knew. In the case of killing that person after that, how will you show your hate? How can you show your hate? Ask these questions to yourself, and you will realize that hate is a personal illusion that is created by you inside your brain. It may or may not have a reason physically existing but, that is irrelevant because hate is an illusion. The reason you stating your hate towards a person may or may not be a real one but, the story, the events, the effects, the visualization, you know those things are happening inside your head that is the reason why I'm telling you, hate, anger, etc., such kind of emotions are personal illusion emotions. And the problem is you will start life in that illusion and, we already know that whatever we are suggesting to our subconscious mind it will absorb. It will show in your life so, if you have that anger, if you have that hate, it will absorb the anger and show that in your life and, that is not good for your goal.

Increase of love and pain you can feel it, see it, here it sometimes you have to talk about it. It will be there no matter whatever the situation is. Because it is real, love and pain are always real. One of the best ways to control all other emotions except love and pain is to make a realization in your heart that whatever you are facing right now is imaginary, once you try to generate that thought whenever you are in anger or, hate or, any such kind of situation or, any such kind of trouble, you will be able to control your emotion, especially the imaginary emotions.

So now you know how to control imaginary emotions by generating the realization that it is imaginary. But the real question that comes here right now is how we can control the real emotions? especially the pain. How can one control the pain? well, it is the biggest question asked by so many people themselves and to other people in day-to-day life. Well, controlling pain is not that easy, the simple answer is you cannot control pain, it is almost impossible to control pain because, for only one reason, it is real. It is not something you imagine to control, not even try to control pain. What can we do then? That's a good question. Even though we cannot control pain, we can learn to adapt and handle it. Yes, that is the solution, remember the first day of your gym or the first day of your military exercise is, horrible right but, you adapted by practice and patience. The pain which you had while taking ten pushups after months you won't even feel after taking a hundred pushups. So, the best way is to make the pain part of your life. Your subconscious mind knows and learns to match up with the pain so learning to adapt to pain is the best way to handle the pain since your atomized goals and steps are with you, you will know or you will have at least a slight idea of where you will face a painful situation so, you can prepare yourself and your mind to adapt the painful situation. The other way is to share the things with your chosen loved ones, don't expect a solution from them but, showing the pain to them will help you to ease the effect of pain that will eventually help you to find a way to adapt to the pain and move forward, become much stronger, mature and goal-oriented. It is a skill that you should develop and even the most important one which plays an important role in success in any line of work. During the process of execution fundamentally, we face somethings else also that is challenges, though now we know how to control illusion emotions and pain, challenges will come but, not everyone will overcome it, why? Because the fact is unlike physics, life only attracts the same forces, money attracts money, love attracts love and, problem attracts problem. Therefore, challenge attracts challenge so, why we cannot overcome the problem? Because you are getting more and more problems along with the challenges and compounded. It becomes unsolvable. The best way to overcome the challenge of the problems that you are facing is to consider it as opportunities, and we know like forces attract like so here opportunity will attract more and more opportunities. when you consider it as an opportunity, it gives you a new goal because every opportunity comes with a goal. Now within the problem, you got a goal to work. As you already know how to start working for a goal, I think it is not that tough for you to achieve the goal and, that goal is the solution for your challenge very easy right, as it is like a nested approach instead of saying something like if you approach your goals in the right way it will come to you now, you are approaching in a most appropriate way that is the nested approach. Here what we got is a goal inside a challenge because we consider the challenge as an opportunity, we have to solve that challenge considering it as an opportunity. So, whenever we have a goal, we have to do the steps which are already said in the first and second chapters. Once you did the challenges will go away moreover, you will learn a few more new things, will get more experience and, you will become a pro in solving your challenges. We are reaching an end to the fundamental requirement for achieving our goals, we have an open mindset, we know how to control emotions, how to handle pain, how to overcome challenges but, do we get a guaranteed outcome all the time? No, there is an important thing that you miss and that is nothing but attitude. Attitude plays a key role in achieving goals without attitude all the hard work and smart work can be considered as a waste of time. It is a skill that can be acquired. The best way to acquire an attitude is to learn from someone who already achieved a similar goal to you. Try to learn from their journey, books, friends, social media, if you are confident enough, you must be confident enough then only you can achieve a goal so you can contact the person directly and have a chat with him. But one thing you should remember when you are following a person, you should learn what are the qualities he or she possess, you are not supposed to just copy down the entire thing done by them. There is another way to develop attitude imagine as you did in the first chapter, we can do something else here, you have to go to a calm place, it can be your room, it can be any other place depends upon you then what you have to do is take a deep breath make your mind empty, imagine about a successful goal achieved you in front of you. The man who is in front of you is very successful, he has everything whatever the goal he wanted to achieve the already achieved. Now he is there to help you. This is going to be your image in the successful version now you'll ask that person how you did this? what you did when you face the challenge? This is what do you call self-image construction, when you construct your self-image within you without any help, you will be able to get a very good answer, a very good attitude, a very good way to approach your life but, this process is time-consuming you cannot just go imagine or create a successful image of you and talk to it. It requires a meditative State of mind to create a trance and you should be in a calm state. You might doubt how can I create my self-image, is it possible to create a self-image? As I told you it is not going to be quick, quick is not an option here so you can image yourself and you can motivate that image you can give self-motivation to it by giving proper affirmation and self-motivation he can develop that person into the right image goal-oriented gold achieved person, talk to that person how he became that person, so you are talking to you inside you to develop the outside you. That is an amazing method, not every people can do it but whoever did it will be successful in their life. I would suggest one more method to develop your attitude is to read books, which teach you about how to develop your attitude. By simply reading, it won't work, make sure that you are applying the techniques that are mentioned in that book as we are doing right now with this book that is the most basic step that will help you to develop your attitude to achieve your goal. Self-help books that will help you to achieve this success. If you don't have the habit of reading a book, please do start. You can start by reading things you like, once you generate the habit of reading you can switch to different materials according to the need. At the end of this book, I will provide my personal experience and my suggestions on how the book helped me. I hope that will help you as well to achieve your goals. These are the basic fundamental ideas required for the execution of your plan, to reach the initial step of your goal from the current position. Once you are fundamentally strong, you will be having tremendous control calm attitude, and a strong desire for a goal. Once you are fundamentally strong and sound then half of the execution of the plan is done. The other half depends on the technical side of the execution of the goal. We will be discussing how the technical side of the execution of any goal-oriented process is equally important as the fundamental process. The first and most important technical skill is time management. Time is time and tide waits for no man so, we need to be two steps ahead of it. So that we can beat it.

Steps for time management

Make a schedule: The schedule is important to have time management. When you make a schedule, you must cover all your day-to-day activities in it. It should not be limited to your goal. It should cover all your activities. Few things to keep in mind that when you make a schedule for the first time, it may not be accurate so, you might need to make some changes. Sometimes you may feel like more time should be spent on your goal in that case, change the schedule accordingly but, do not stuff your schedule with activities. There must be flexibility to move around in case any changes need to be applied. The point is if you are not finishing the tasks is also ok but, you have to do the tasks anyway.

Grouping of tasks: Another effective way of managing time is the grouping of the task. How is the grouping of the task that important? It helps you to make sure that you processed the tasks according to schedule. It doesn't mean that only important task needs to be arranged. Other tasks can also be included. It will help you to conserve time and, you won't feel fatigued while working also, setting a reminder for tasks according to the schedule will improve time management.

Taking rewards: One of the effective ways to have time management is to reward yourself. Keep small, small rewards such as if you completed three important tasks then you will eat a bar of chocolate, or you will spend time with your loved ones. You can talk about this to your chosen and loved ones and set some reward such as if you complete everything as per the schedule you and your partner will go and have a dance, etc. You may set a lot of funny rewards that will motivate you, that will give you enough strength, energy to do your work in a scheduled manner.

There might be other ways also but, these are the ways that I found useful and efficient. If you have any other better ways, you can also apply that. The point is technically in time management, we should be able to beat the time if you are capable of doing it first part of the technical requirement is done.

Now the next important part is knowledge because knowledge plays a very, very, very important role.

How to gather knowledge?

Social media: In the current scenario, the best way to get knowledge about your goal is through social media such as YouTube, Facebook, Instagram, WhatsApp groups, etc. you should keep in mind that in social media, the knowledge can be misleading as well so be brave enough to take the data from the legitimate sources also do not have everything to your heart, check out the knowledge and create your perspective that suits your goal.

News and article: Even though social media are the dynamic and most powerful media right now, we should not leave behind our conventional form of information in newspaper articles, magazines, extra. Have a collection of it. Most of it will be legit, which is one advantage but do not take every stuff, only the required pieces of the knowledge.

Books: Which plays a very important role in collecting knowledge. Read books, for example, the book you're reading right now, it is good right. So, selecting the books which give you the right knowledge and perception about the outcome of you are the goal. One important thing that you should keep in mind while reading a book is you should be consistent because a book has that positivity that will help you to keep your mind refreshed so if you're reading a book doesn't matter which book you are reading make sure that you read consistently to achieve your greatest goals.

Mentor: This is very important, having a mentor is good for you, for your growth, anyone or anything can be a coach but if you have a mentor how will maybe a YouTuber, Scientist, books, etc. he will be able to guide you in a lot in your goal-achieving process. In my personal experience, I consider the books that I used to read as my mentor and their works. I used to follow their findings teachings books, and videos articles everything that keeps me motivated as well as the goal-oriented success of any process even the Jesus Christ had his own at work that's why he is so powerful if you read the bible, you will see that how he transformed it.

How to create a network?

Social media is the best tool we have right now for networking. Create your network in it. It is a kind of necessity, always remember networking is a process in which you need to interact with people, not just follow and like once you form a circle of people having the same kind of mindset and goals, it will help you to move faster and more efficient way.

Networking is communicating so, do not miss any opportunity to communicate your view and perception. Also, keep in mind that whatever the receiver's reply, you be on the positive side while networking the one thing you all are going to see is rejection so, you do not worry about rejection instead enjoy it, celebrate it, and learn from it. The next most important factor in any goal-oriented process is nothing but finances. Yes, finances are required. For every process, you may think that to achieve the goal of becoming a millionaire. You don't have million dollars, that is completely ok. To be a millionaire, you need millions but, to start your process, you just need a mindset of getting the first $1, then you can make a million billion or more.

How to create finances?

Creating finances is a humongous task. Maybe in the future, when this book helped you reach the initial step of your goal, I will be writing a book on finances exclusively. Here I will be providing a few must-following methods for having the financial outcome.

- Investing 50 percent of your total income in a good investment plan would at least provide a return that will help you to have a financially stable life over some time.
- Keep a schedule for your expenses and, deleting unnecessary expenses from the period will make you strong in terms of finances.
- 10 percent of your total income should be saved for emergency purposes. no matter what, only for emergency needs, related to your goal, you are going to touch it.
- Spend enough money so that you don't feel depressed economically and enjoy your life. It will improve your quality of earning.
- Avoid keeping money stagnant either spend or invest except the emergency fund.
- Stick to your financial plan even though it might show some lack of accuracy. Also, update the plan, if necessary, with the new types of investments and programs after a thorough study and financial advice.
- Do not change or alter your financial plan based on your stupid emotions. I hope you don't do those things after reading this book.

By combining the fundamentals and technical, you will be ready to execute your goal efficiently. These are the basic steps and preparations required for you to reach the initial point of your goal or the change needed to achieve the goal. I remind you of one thing at this moment, these are not the steps to achieve your goal these are ways, that you will correct your path to reach the initial point of your ultimate goal. By following these methods, if you reach your goal, I am so happy but, I believe few other things also need to be taken care of to achieve the ultimate goal. The coming chapters will be discussed.

FOUR
FAITH

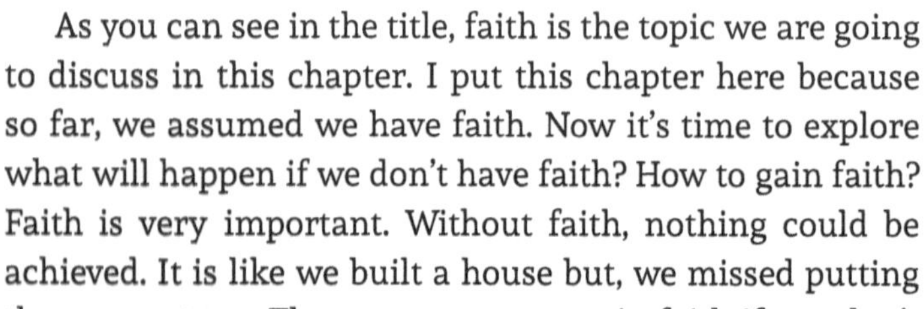

As you can see in the title, faith is the topic we are going to discuss in this chapter. I put this chapter here because so far, we assumed we have faith. Now it's time to explore what will happen if we don't have faith? How to gain faith? Faith is very important. Without faith, nothing could be achieved. It is like we built a house but, we missed putting the cornerstone. There are ways to attain faith if you don't have it. There are ways to retain faith if it is required. We will be discussing all of it in this chapter.

First, what is faith?

Well, there are a lot of ways one can define faith. Someone will say faith is something or some belief that we should have on something or someone. I'm was not satisfied with that definition. I believe faith is some belief in yourself, in your thing. If our belief is in someone else, we require his or her help to achieve our goal. If faith is the belief in someone else, how can we sure that we are following the right person. How can we sure that we are working hard on our goal if we don't believe in ourselves. If you do not have faith in yourself, no matter how talented, smart and, goal-oriented you are, nothing great is going to happen. Some might say we should have faith in God. Of course, we must have faith in God. God also said your body is the temple of God. So, it means you should believe in yourself. Belief in yourself is a must-have thing to acquire faith. Once you have the right amount of faith clubbed with the desire that you already have then, do not worry about other things. It will be taken care of by your subconscious mind. You have to carry on with your plan according to your desire with faith.

Now assuming you do not have faith, we will try to attain faith, or we will be looking into different ways to attain the faith.

How to attain faith?

There are several ways to attain faith. I believe there are some must-follow steps through that anyone can attain faith.

By search: Search is a method by which we can attain faith in our life. Nowadays, we love to google search for everything we could search for faith, not in google but in real life. Search for the people, institutions, and communities that already attained faith or on the path of success in attaining it. Like I already said in the previous chapter, in life, the same forces attract each other. When you search for the wisdom of faith, it will come to you. You will find mentors and people who can induce faith in you. When you, searching for the faith you will learn it through results. The more you search, you will see more results, which are attained only because of huge faith. Your search for faith can be started by start reading a book, which is written by eminent personalities who attained their dreams only because of strong faith. Once the wisdom of faith comes in contact with you, drastic changes will happen.

By Motivation: Personally, I'm not that great fan of motivation instead I believe in coaching them. But I do accept the fact that motivation helps you to find faith. You may ask how? Well, psychologically motivation creates an aura of "feeling better" around you for few minutes or may be months and years. The point is you have a hell lot of positive auras around you at the moment. Once you have a positive aura around you, the best thing you could improvise is to concentrate it to a point. In our case it will be yourself. More clearly you should focus the aura within yourself. By doing this exercise along with correct pristine motivation, you will feel special, capable and powerful. This feeling will open a door for all the positive attraction. What you have to do is to accept and fix it in your mind. All the positivity. Over a period of time, you will start reflecting positivity all around and that is the point where faith is born in you to yourself. It actually works this way but the problem is you have to motivate yourself every time because it won't last forever. Like a medicine, you should intake the positivity of motivation in periodic basis.

By Results: Another wat you attain faith is by seeing results. It will work in two ways, either the faith will come to you or you will attain it by seeing other's results or by seeing your own results. Well, seeing other's we already discussed in the beginning. Faith can be attained by our own results. It can be done in two ways. First one, you have to visualize the result. Since we followed the steps in this book, you knew the result and every minute steps through which goal can be achieved. So, you can visualize.

Initially you may not feel it as convincing, but you should visualize, doing repeatedly over a period of time the results and its steps will get embedded in the subconscious mind. Once it is embedded you will start to feel different, you will start to address faith, you will start to believe. That will work wonders for you. Secondly, assume you have the clear idea about your goal and like in the above section if you are motivated enough, you will start achieving small, small goal. Due to the small, small victories your faith in yourself will also increase. Whenever a task is completed, our brain will send a message "Task completed by following steps" to subconscious mind. Eventually the subconscious mind will be attracted towards your goal and your ability that will increase your faith drastically. These small steps and ways are our path for an amazing life.

These are the few steps that I found it effective to build your faith. In conclusion, it all depends on the suggestion you have given to the subconscious mind. Now we are going to take a look at how to retain our faith.

How to retain faith?

Once you have faith or once you attain faith it means your mindset and brain pattern conditioned to the particular state. It is started to have a conviction over faith. So, retaining faith is very important. It is not a difficult task to retain faith. Th funny side is if you lost faith in certain things then it will be very difficult to get it back. I will explain it in the later part, to get back lost faith.

Now the best ways to retain faith is by:

Consistent work

Consistent work is one of the best ways to retain faith. Once you have a plan and started executing it, you will be following the methods which is developed by our previous methods or any methods, assuming you have faith already, if not follow the steps in the first part of the chapter. Coming to our point, once you are started working with methods, you are actually practicing the methods and we all know practice makes a person perfect. So, the chances of getting results are not less than hundred percent. Once you do consistent work, it will open up new possibilities automatically because your brain pattern is lined up to follow the path. So, anything happening against it will be blocked by your subconscious mind and that will help the faith to get indulge more and more into our pattern.

Celebrations

Celebrations are very powerful tool to retain faith. Without celebration life is as same as dead. Celebrations are not always throwing a party to friends. Celebrations can be the moment that you feel really high in satisfaction and joy. Whenever you are reached that state, you have to embrace it. There are lots of ways to celebrate your small and big success, all those feelings will get automatically absorbed in the subconscious mind. Subconscious mind will use this as a fuel to invest in faith. Eventually faith will increase, and it will get retained. Again, I'm reminding you small or big success or even failure, celebrate because either it will teach you to do something right or you already did something great. Both are fertilizer for faith.

Fame

The next one is fame. Yes, this is a real deal of retaining faith. Everybody wants to become famous, recognition, we do all sort of things to become famous. All this YouTube, Instagram, tik tok, etc... are the medium used to become famous or trying to get attention of others. The companies know this psychological phenomenon, that craving of humans to becomes famous and they supported with the right platform, it is a win-win for both of us. Now the question is how it will help? A goal obviously will attract some sort of fame or recognition, so it will attract more people it and these people will observe you, try to follow you, try to learn from you. That means they have some faith you or else faith in the method that you are following. As we already know subconscious mind will take suggestions from anywhere so faith on you will act as a heterogeneous suggestion to retain your faith.

How to boost faith?

Clarity of vision: By following the steps provided in the previous chapters, you will be in the right path. The more you travel through the right path, your vision become clearer to you. A brighter vision is always acting as a faith booster. It works as a feedback such as You followed your own method that make your vision clear, so you will tend believe in the method that you follow that will boost your faith. There are some other important elements which makes your vision clear that is nothing but imagination and repetition. Clarity of your vision also brings calmness to your life because your vision knows the result, so it doesn't matter the in-between events. That calmness again boosts your faith. Faith gained by clarity of vision is clubbed with amazing enthusiasm. Since you are aware of your end result and pathways, you will be eager to work on it. Even though you have enough enthusiasm I recommend you follow all the required steps to do things.

By more results: when you are getting more and more successful results, you automatically believe in your plan or process that you are executing. Even if by luck or something you are getting result that will act as catalyst to boost your faith in yourself. Results have the magical power to keep you in track. No matter what the challenges, hardships or odds. If we are getting result obviously, we will be happy, and that happiness will again boost your faith. Results also have the power of compound effect. Because result will give an outcome to you as well as some other people, so they will start showing respect and believe in you so their faith also increased, your faith also increasing thus it get compounded. The only drawback of result-oriented faith is we might develop a feeling of super pro, well that is not good. Well, we will become pro, but it should be said by others not by ourselves. So that you should be careful otherwise your attitude will shift and the faith pattern in subconscious brain will be broken. You may ask why subconscious mind do that? My answer is whatever it may, it is none of our business. All we have to care is not to get carried away by our results. Over a period of time your results will go exponential that will help you to grow your faith in exponentially as well. Finally, you will become an aura of positivity and a true example of true faith.

Purpose of life: This is real yet most abstract way of improving or boosting your faith. Purpose, whatever we do, we do with an intention. Here the funny fact is whatever we do is always positive. Positivity attracts faith. When you set a goal and move forward in your life, you will understand the purpose of life in some point. A planned approach will always show purpose of life. Once your plan shows the purpose of your life, your subconscious mind has no choice other than believe in it. By the way the message needs to be feed to subconscious via conscious mind. Purpose boost faith in your life. Because purpose is something most of the people fail to figure out. Here, you did it. You know your purpose, what is required faith, so there is only one choice to attain enough faith and shows an extraordinary belief system. Now we will be looking into how to get back the faith that we lost due to any reason in the next session.

How to regain faith?

The next main thing that we should look into it is, what we should we do if we lose faith? What should we do if we lose faith completely? Well to be honest, if you are following whatever written in this book and also the things which is mentioned in the coming chapters, I'm sure that you will not lose your faith. Either you will gain faith, or you will retain faith. Still if somehow, we lost faith the below steps may help.

Spirituality

Being spiritual is one of the best and easy way to

gain faith which is lost. No matter what religion you follow, being religious have nothing to do with spirituality. Once you read and follow the teachings of spiritual coaches and teachers, you will have higher chance to take back the lost faith. The reason why I insist on spiritual coach is because you just lost not failed yet. You will only fail in your life when you lose the spirit of game. Normally our mind and body will be in balance by spirituality and that is the reason why I stated. The one thing you should keep in mind that when you. Regain faith via spirituality for that few days you are not supposed to think or do anything else, our ultimate goal is to regain faith. You may use any book or this book to make your path and the steps to design your spiritual method you wanted to follow.

Meditation

Meditation has a larger effect in regain the lost faith. When you meditate your mind and body will come to its balance. This is the only thing which leads to keep faith by doing meditation. There are lots of other ways as well I hope you always aware of that. So do not wait until you lose faith to start meditation. You may make it as a part of your life by doing 10-15 minutes both morning and night if possible, evening also.

Self-motivation

Self-motivation is the best motivation. Once you're good enough to motivate yourself that itself will vibrate your subconscious mind to regain the faith that you lost. But the question you might ask here is, how anyone could motivate himself If he already lost faith? There we have to use a little trick. Do you remember our chosen one, those who should be in us to our success? You may lose faith, but those people won't and they never do. It's your responsibility for keep their faith in you. Your primary key for self-motivation is them. It means you will have someone to keep you motivated self by showing their faith in you. Once the self-motivation kicks in cultivate it for your faith and harvest it.

Proper sleep.

The last thing to regain faith is proper sleep. It might sound crazy but proper sleep will have the effect of getting your faith back. Scientifically our body tends to o sleep when we lost, or we are in depression or not in a good mood. This is how our body tries to revive internally, removes all the negative dangerous pattern from the body. But we humans once wake up again we again dwell in the past, that is our hobby. Instead, what you have to do is try few consistent proper sleeps this time it will be quicker and efficient. You will obviously observe changes happening in you if you sleep consistently peacefully irrespective of situation. That will automatically help you to form a pathway to regain faith in you. These are the few ways I found useful and effective there could be many ways but trust me these ways will definitely help you.

In the coming lessons we will be discussing on other factors which plays important roles in reaching the path we wanted.

FIVE

SEX

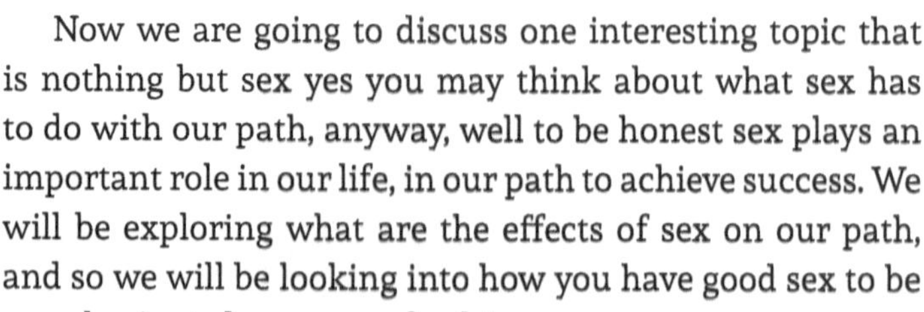

Now we are going to discuss one interesting topic that is nothing but sex yes you may think about what sex has to do with our path, anyway, well to be honest sex plays an important role in our life, in our path to achieve success. We will be exploring what are the effects of sex on our path, and so we will be looking into how you have good sex to be a goal-oriented person and achieve success.

Before looking into that, let's check the physiological psychological effect of having sex.

Considering you are having good sex, You know how to do it. Internally in our body what will happen is hypothalamus will respond to sexual arousal it will produce testosterone which is a hormone another home is dopamine which plays a vital role in sexual attraction and the euphoric feeling while having sex and there are several other hormones as well as other things happening inside our body having sex. I do not want to go to it since I was biology student years ago, I just mention a few hormones to show off. The point is when having good sex, you tend to forget yourself and due to the secretion of different chemicals inside your body your metabolic activity tends to increase the metabolism increases it tends to give you refreshment it helps to free you and your body, and it fulfills a basic human need. Indirectly in psychology also get the effect of the secretion and hormones will take place since we are trying to move out of a real-world it reset the brain especially brain pattern in your head what is the brain reset? What would happen? We get a new, fresh pattern to set and modified according to our wishes. Since due to higher metabolic activity inside the body most of the nerves and connections will get excited, and the effect will last for days, what do you have to do is to follow the rules and steps which are given in the previous chapters and create new connections in this time? It can do wonders, there is another hormone called vasopressin it is the hormone that causes aggression and stress, having good sex will suppress the production of this hormone that keeps you able to handle yourself and keep your calm and also help you to get out of the stressful feeling. Sex work as a helping hand, auto catalyst That not only helps to reset the brain pattern but also helps to keep you in control of your unwanted unreal emotions such as anger as well.

Now, list checks a few things that are required to have proper sex.

Desire to have sex.

The desire for good sex is required not because you read the book, then you think that let's go and have sex. No, it does not work like that. You should have a strong desire for sex and the feelings behind it. It is not a medicine, but it can cure lots of problems.

Love partner

The sex, the sex which I mentioned here is no rough sex it is the sex which comes with the love of your partner this is the one reason I initially choose wife or girlfriend as the chosen one sex without the feeling of love is just action of time pass and action of time pass don't give you the result you want. You want to make your targets into results, you have to do sex with the right person with the right feeling.

Timing of sex

This is a very important aspect, without proper timing sex won't work. It is good timing in the sense of the time of having sex. Time your sex and other partner availability and your timing everything should be in an amendment it varies from person to person, do not force yourself or your partner into it. Because you won't get your goal by force. First, you should be generating the feeling internally, then you should give you time to get into a pattern of having good sex.

Be genuine.

Be genuine, do not try anything extra when having sex that you do not know how to execute. If you are facing any problem, discuss it with your partner this is the problem that I am facing but do not fake it. Faking particular things like sex, love, your nature, attitude, everything will have a negative effect on you. Here, we don't want any negativity on you, what we need is positivity. My heart is genuine, we will be able to do everything right eventually.

Several ways that we can have a good sexual life what were the concerns that come with a sexual life stay faithful and love your partner discuss among your so what are the concerns that you're facing because sex as a catalyst to our success is very much important in everyone's life. So is significant in your life as well. In the coming chapters, we will discuss more other particular things that we usually don't discuss in any books to have a success.

SIX

INTENSITY OF MOOD

I thought of putting this chapter as part of another chapter, but suddenly my thoughts changed this is going to be a very small chapter the idea that I wanted to convey here is very small, but most of the time this particular session is not discussed anywhere in any book. So here I wanted to tell you something about the intensity of mood.

The intensity of mood is a phenomenon that is experienced by everyone every time. I will divide this into two. The first one is intensity and the second one is mood intensity means the power or amount of a particular thing or substance, such as intensity of light extra. Mood means, which is an internal state represented by a human while he is infected or affected by the external factor. It can be a good mood, bad mood, crazy mood, etc. Whatever the mood we have, our activities are always based on the intensity or power of mood. Let's take an example, consider you are going to buy a car you follow the steps nested down the pros and the cons finally arrive at the initial step, the initial point of your path to reach the goal from your current state that is to buy a car theoretically. Once you start executing the steps may be while you are choosing the color of your favorite car, you hear that your best friend or your colleague or someone had some accident, or some issue has happened so at that particular moment what will happen is your mood that will change. Doesn't matter whatever you are doing till that moment is nothing because just your mood got changed. It does happen with every person, it can happen in any situation because our intensity and our pattern of mood are very important.

Your intensity of mood can be affected by internal as well as external factors, what is the factor it maybe once the intensity of the energy that you carry forward while you are in a particular mood if it is distracted or distorted in some way the thing that you do will not reach the correct point. You may have a full-fledged plan you may have the resources at your disposal, you may have everything planned, steps everything will be there for you but the intensity of doing a particular thing is very essential if the thing is like your life the thing that you cannot live without so things you have an internal effect of mood in your life. For example, it's you want to build a multi-story house a building that is like life without that you cannot die peacefully. You have everything for that and what happened was like when you started working on it everything is sorted for you, you have the plan, you have the money, you have the resources, you have everything but suddenly what happened due to any some factors due to some issues or due to some other issues which is not related to your goal because of that your internal state of mindset got hurt. Your mind, it got changed, your temperament got changed. In those scenarios your mindset or mind pattern got affected because of the internal issues which are happening inside you there are certain other factors which are affected your intensity of mood externally those factors are like maybe an issue with your parent or maybe any negative things which are happening outside which are got an interaction with your goal with your plan and that struggles mind change mindset change inside you without you knowing. In our example of choosing the color of the car, you possibly continue choosing the color of the car after hearing the bad news of accident or the death which is caused to your colleague you will continue to choose the color of the car, but the point is the intensity that you carry to choose right before the event and after the event is different. Since the intensity of the mood changed your mood is actually changed so what will happen is the colour that you can pick before the event and after the event can be different doesn't mean that a hundred percent it will be different now, it can be different 80 % of the time. Please be aware once the trigger of negative energy happens inside your mind it will multiply just as positive energy, so keeping your mood and its intensity at most positive is very important.

The intensity of mood is not a thing that anyone can teach you, it is something that we derive according to a situation both physically and psychologically internally and externally.

So, I just want to inform you that even though you have everything at your disposal if you don't have a good mood it can affect your goal it can be in a small negligible way or can be in a drastic catastrophic way. So, the point is to keep your mood and its intensity always high and positive, whatever is required to do. If you follow the steps are mentioned earlier in the book and consider the intensity of mood is your goal, we can achieve that point by doing meditations by reading books keeping your workspace away from all the distractions, and a lot of other things that can be done, so I hope this particular chapter, give you a procession about your mood. Most of the people when you do things people won't consider external factors that is true, we don't have to consider external factors that going to hurt our goal, but it can impact internally without our knowledge and where it will affect us? It is in the intensity of doing or things.

SEVEN
WORK AREA

Work area is one of major part of any goal-oriented person. There are a few things that everyone should follow as part of work area etiquette. Most of the parts mentioned in the chapter you might already know, but doesn't matter, we are here to make sure that everything followed thoroughly.

Work area is nothing but the place where you're going to sit and develop your path and goal. Theoretically, this place you should consider as sacred, because this is the place where your roots for the future is going to develop. We must keep it proper.

How to set up a work area?

- Choose a clean spot which would be away from other disturbances. Since, you are going to work there you should keep it as private, nothing apart from your goal is happening there
- Make sure you have good table space and chair setup
- Make sure there is proper sunlight and proper ventilation

- If you are a meditative person, make sure you have enough space for meditation as well.
- If you are spiritually sound, make sure you have a proper prayer area within your work area. You may keep holy books and other related stuff there.
- Proper light arrangement and positive fragrance should be there.
- You should consider this as your personal development area and should not do any other things there.
- Should have enough space to keep your books, laptop and other things required for your goal.
- Should have a clock or timepiece in the room. We don't want to check the phone for time and divert into notifications and so on.
- Keep all the necessary stationary for easy access
- If you could set at least the above-mentioned things, then it would be an ideal work area to build goals and path.

Etiquette that should follow in a work area.

- Should keep it clean and positive fragrance such as lemon, rose should be there. The moment you enter into the room, you should feel to work from there.
- While working try to look professional, it doesn't mean that you should wear a suit, what ever you wear should be clean and tidy.
- Pray before start working and do not take any past sorrows with you, while praying make sure you thank more than you ask.

- Keep a ledger or diary of all your work, it is your personal experience encyclopedia. This will help you to guide yourself in similar situation, as well as help you to guide others to the path of success once you reach the goal.
- Do not sleep on your work area, if you are tired go to your bedroom and sleep for few minutes.
- Do not let anyone other than your chosen ones to interfere in any settings in the work area.
- Do not let any distractions in your work area that might have a negative impact on your intensity of mood.
- You don't have to show your work area to everyone, instead show them your result.

By keeping a proper work area and following the work area etiquette, your process of goal will be faster and efficient. The positive aura surrounding the work area will help you to get through minor setbacks as well.

There are a lot of other ways to keep the work area amazing and useful.

EIGHT

MOMENT OF RESULT

Moment of result is a phenomenon that everybody in their life will experience. This amazing phenomenon might change a lot of things in and out of your life. I initially thought of putting this chapter last, then I thought if a person is following my book and the materials suggested by me, then he should not wait until the end to know, how the feeling of result would be.

Every moment of result will change something or the other, it is the moment where all your hard work that raised hard questions will get an answer. This is the time when you realize, you feel blessed and superior. The moment the people who treated you stupid start to respect you. The moment may be a fraction of a second in your entire life but the moment going to impact your entire life both past and future. The feeling of satisfaction we get at that time is unimaginable, and it cannot be easily described by words. Each day you wake up and hustle, again and again, you follow the same thing and in one split second, the most awaited result will come. That second is the most important time in your life, even if you are going to die at that moment also there would not be any regret and your heart will be filled with happiness and love.

The moment o result is very influential, that moment will contain the purpose, reason, ambition, your training everything you did to achieve the particular result. That exact moment is the point where others call an overnight success. The exact moment you proved your method, path, and all the steps are right.

While you visualize your future, you must be able to visualize your moment of the result as well, which is very significant. Because all your success and its visibility to the outer world will come from this point only. The world is actually going to see the success from you on this exact point. So the moment of result or the moment of giving result mixed with your imagination will help the brain to reach your necessary point faster than you ever think.

NINE

REJECTED SOUL

Sometimes if we work hard also, we might not get the result we are looking for. Let's say you have the vision of building some kind of business, and you sat down and theoretically deduced a plan to execute, you did all the necessary changes and followed the instructions to reach the initial point of your path to reach your goal, but when you present the plan to the clients or the people you thought worth sharing, and they will reject you, they all started rejecting you. You tried to see as many as possible but nothing great is happening, all of them are simply rejecting you and this is how you become a rejected soul. This point is very important, this is a kind of test for you to assess yourself as well as it is the time to prove how good you are fundamental. The inner strength of you actually matters here the most. Being rejected is hard, but you may do a lot of that can actually do wonders over a period of time. Once, I will be pointing out what is the common state of mind you will have. Once you got rejected multiple times also, I will help you how to react and adapt to the situation and work accordingly. To be honest, being rejected is good.

Once you are getting rejections continuously, most of the time you would think in the following ways:

- You would be thinking that fundamentally there might be a problem with you.
- You might think that you are not worthy of anything, all these are just dreams.
- Likewise, you might fall into depression
- You might think my method was not correct, not meant for you.
- You may feel ill and unable to think and do anything else.
- Furthermore, you may stick in the loop, never feel happy.
- Besides, you may feel like you are a big-time loser and garbage.
- You will lose your beliefs and start to lack faith.
- You might face family concerns as well because of your rejected mindset.
- Likewise, you may start to hate God and feel terrible, might go out of the zone of prayers as well.
- You might run away from all the dreams and feel terrible and live with regret.

These are the few commonly seen attitude or states of mind or the way people approach life once they got rejected. But I do not want anyone in the entire world to be like this because we have seen so many people become winners, revolutionists capable of changing the world after facing a lot of rejections. If you are getting rejected frequently, I want you to follow the below points that will help you.

- If you are getting rejected, do not think of it as a failure. It is just feedback, collect the feedback and analyze and adjust accordingly from the data or conclusion drawn from that feedback.

- Do not get depressed, instead celebrate your rejections. You may wonder, how can anyone celebrate rejections? Well, it depends on how you think. If you think like I got rejected today, then you started thinking like I'm not good, then you will end up in depression. Instead of that you may think as today I have learned that there is being some issue with my plan, I need to analyze it, by this approach it is not working, so I need to step up my level and work on it, maybe I need to check with someone who can give me a few mentorships in this way you will think out of the box when you think out of the box your brain will open up to new perceptions and ideas that is more than you to celebrate. Celebrations will keep negativity away from you. Even if it is a small rejection, celebrate it, it will help you to keep your enthusiasm and positivity intact.
- Another way to keep you quiet even if you are rejected is by keeping you are intensity of mood intact.
- Mostly when you face extreme rejection you may start to think in weird ways, when you find extreme rejection stop for a while what you are doing right now, relax a bit, and then find a good life coach or a mentor if possible, remember it is for extreme rejections, like when you are about to suicide kind of situation.
- Start loving rejections it is a part of life it happens there are a lot of problems that happen like that it is completely ok not the end of the world not the end of opportunities.
- Practice making a man perfect we all know that, so practice the way of communication appearance attitude, etc. so that you may avoid future rejection.

- Start to see rejections as a blessing, keep on trying to learn from them, there will be a day not later for you to achieve your dreams.
- As I mentioned in our previous chapters challenges actually opportunities so here, first you need to consider rejections, how the challenges happened because of rejections has new opportunities build a plan accordingly using the method which is given in this book, work it out it will definitely work.
- Do not suppress the emotions whatever you feel, you want to cry then cry nothing wrong with that it cools you down, cools your mind.

There are a few more qualities that rejection can give you if you are taking rejection as a positive element

- It will make you stronger and sharper
- It will improve your communication skills and analytical skills.
- Furthermore, it will give you good customer knowledge and the skills to improve you as a person.
- It will make your mind pattern flexible and more powerful, you will be able to read a person the moment you see him.
- It improves your vision and does not let any unnecessary hopes in your mind

These are the few things I felt rejections can give you or make you as a person you follow good, and the goodwill eventually follow you in the coming chapters will discuss more our requirement to develop ourselves as a person as a goal-oriented man and other stuff too.

TEN
DREAMS

Dreams are always the most important part of a man's life, in fact, dreams are the foundation of everything. The cars, computers, the gadgets, even this book is a result of a dream. I put this chapter here because so far, we assumed we are clear about our dreams. So just in case if you are not clear about your dreams this chapter will definitely help you to make it clear.

The dreams which can be divided into two types, the one which comes to our mind while sleeping and the other one which does not allow us to sleep until it is achieved. Both these dreams are critical, both have its own significance in our life. In this chapter, we will look into the dreams that doesn't allow us to sleep. These are the set of dreams that we would love to achieve in our life, these are the set of dreams that fulfills the purpose of our life. It can be any materialistic or non-materialistic thing that varies from person to person. But the thing that usually people mistake with the dream is nothing but its purpose. Yes, what is the purpose of any dream? Why we have this dream? Lot of such kind of questions, first we will discuss the purpose of dream, let's say you wanted to buy a super car, which is very expensive, that's your dream car, you are doing everything possible to buy the car but nothing happening, no matter what you do nothing is happening. Do you know why this is not happening, it is because of a simple equation mismatch, this might be your dream, car but is it fulfil your purpose of your life, or is it linked with any purpose of the life, Is that dream in your head because others have the super car, you just need to show off to others that I have this kind of car, or it's really linked to any purpose? Let's take another scenario, one other guy just like you, he wanted a super car he started planning to achieve it, let's say his time frame 2 years, he works smart but the difference in his case, every time he is doing it is always linked to e-commerce business, it means all of his plan whether it failed or not failed it is always linked to the e-commerce business. That means the purpose of his dream to have a super car is to build a well-established business. That will financially help him, maybe help so many others. The point I wanted to make here is you will not be able to achieve any dream which not linked with your dream. So, either we need to select something to do which is linked with your passion to life, or your dream should be something which reveals the purpose of your life. It is next to impossible to select a work flow that is connected to the purpose of your life, we cannot say this is the purpose of your life, so you should do this. Then what we should do? Here is the magical power of the dream. The more you want your dream to be reality, the more it will push you and reveal your true purpose, you may drop the plan of super car, but definitely it will give you much better things that satisfy your desire, this is why dream is so important.

Your dream must be real, the emotions attached to it must be real, it can be illogical, but the dream must be real.

The more your dream is real, the more it will attract, the more it attracts, the more it will clear your vision as well. The clearer your vision the more it will push the purpose of your life, The dream, vision and purpose will align in perfect harmony then whatever required to do to achieve it will take time of blink of an eye. So far, we have discussed how dream going to be, why it is required and such things, now we will be looking on to something very interesting how to make the dream a reality. Visualization is the only thoughtful way to make any dream reality. For example, for having a super, visualizing about owning a super car is required but the visualizing the path to achieve is more important. When you want a clear path visualize backwards, start from result then visualize backwards step by step. Once you get a picture don't stop there, feel it, mix it with your real emotions, the path will; become very clear.

Few tips to follow to enhance the path and dream:

- Meditation, doing meditation for few minutes daily will help you to visualize more clearly
- Writing down what exactly appearing in the mind and try to form steps by connecting the fragments will create the vision much better.
- Dreams should be in a way that we already achieved it, use as much as energy to make it very realistic
- Talk about your dream to yourself think in different dimension focus on what stopping you, make a plan using the previous chapter to get rid of it.
- Always keep a positive attitude even in the worst of the worst situation

- Assess all you work in a day-to-day basis, have a calculation how far you are from your dream. Work smarter to make it clearer, that will help you to connect the missing links and get a clear picture.

The dream is a bigger topic to discuss, I tried my best to segregate what is important for a real hustler.

ELEVEN

KNOWING HOPE

Hope is a feeling it is an amazing feeling, not everyone will understand it, but everyone will experience it in life. Trigger of hope is another incredible thing in our life, every moment of hope is triggered by either positive or negative events in life. Unfortunately, so many people that I came across use hope as a place to hide, that is not hope, that is wishful thinking, though it gives us motivation, it does not help us to build our life.

If you are a truly hopeful man, then it will help in many ways:

- Hope helps us to know about the surrounding with more peace
- Hope helps to understand the people around us.
- It keeps us boosted and guided irrespective of the situation
- Hope holds our emotions and keeps us in equilibrium.
- Hope is the reason why most of us are happy to see you tomorrow.

We will be discussing furthermore detail their points and adding a few to the list in the following chapter.

Hope is very magical, it can come to our lives in so many ways, in fact, hope is always there, we will get its experience in so many ways. Hope is the point where our perception takes deviations without any reason. There is no human being living in the world without hope. Even the dumbest fellow on the earth has a bit of hope. I heard a lot of people saying "that was my last hope" "I'm done" these things are stupid. There is no such thing as last hope. If something did not work as you thought, then your approach needs to be changed. The important thing to keep in mind when there is a discussion about hope is nothing but prayer with faith. Prayer with faith is a significant element in hope, Prayer is what brings spiritual energy that cements the faith and reality of something, that will produce hope. Small setbacks or some negative reviews will not hurt you, instead, you will find a new way or much more efficient way to solve the problem and achieve what you want to achieve. When prayer, faith, and hope to come in aligned, our conscious and subconscious will be in the best harmony to attract the right things exactly at the right time.

Now we will discuss something about the dirty work of hope, actually, it's not that hope is dirty, people around us make it dirty. Religious institutions, human Gods, everyone using the weakness of man and selling hope to us. And people somehow get lured into it. What we should understand is we cannot buy hope, neither we can sell. My dear friends, do not fall into these traps. Real hope is inside you. You have to open the door to let the hope uplift you into greater heights. Trust yourself, pray for yourself, have faith in what you do and what you believe. The door of hope will open so that you can stay away from all these dirty works done by dirty eyes by using hope. Your hope is in you, your hope is you.

Few things that we could see only in hopeful man:

- He will have a glow in the eyes, glow of perception, vision, and mission
- He will not give up, always have a way to do things if there is a setback, he knows something new
- Fear will not be there, but faith and respect will be seen in all his actions.
- He will not be tiered in his actions, neither he will feel alone because hope will be there to help.
- He will not try to do anything stupid; he will not search for any shortcuts. Furthermore, he has the correct way, the right path, he may already know what this book is all about.
- Hopeful man has no sad days, he may experience pain, but he knows the answer.
- Hopeful man is the man of calmness and patience, we will see the difference in him the moment we see.

TWELVE
LOVE YOURSELF

Since you are aware of your goal, the importance of hope, faith, and all other elements, you should have also be aware of the importance of loving yourself. Love yourself, Greatest of love is loving yourself, you should feel the aura carried by love, then only you would be able to love others. Most of the people I saw, forgot to love themselves. They will be running for jobs, working hard for the family, and a lot of other stuff will be there on their head. For me personally, if there is no love on me by me, I felt like I'm doing some crime. Self-love is very important; we may have a thousand work to do, but without self-love whatever we achieve will eventually give us some regrets. All the hard work and pain will be nothing if there is no self-love. Love is the greatest joy in life, without love nothing possible, whatever we built, it is not just for money or good status in society, it is for the love, in order to build something for love with love you should know how to love yourself. When I say love yourself, it not only means taking care of yourself but also a divine feeling that is experienced inside you. There is a power of feelings and peace will be there, self-love is the picture of the power of the subconscious mind. The more you're aligned with subconscious and conscious, the more you have love towards yourself. It's the harmony between two reflects in you. Self-love brings you happiness, immense happiness. If you have love towards you, the happiness will radiate to those who surround you as well. Since your belief, faith hope, conscious and subconscious in alignment we could say God is in you, therefore, the happiness radiates by self-love is of God's aura, that's magical and unimaginable, but we could experience and enjoy.

If you have all the things in the world that you wanted to have and your priority is family, then self-love is a must. Take a look at this "Ephesians 5:33 Nevertheless let every one of you in particular so love his wife even as himself; and the wife sees that she reverences her husband" No matter what you gift, whatever places you take her what matters is how much you love yourself, it's clearly written that wife see that she reverences her husband, it's about how you treat yourself, then only you can reflect what you have.

Now take a look at this "1 Corinthians 13:1-6 KJV: Though I speak with the tongues of men and of angels, and have not charity, I have become as sounding brass, or a tinkling cymbal. And though I have the gift of prophecy, and understand all mysteries, and all knowledge; and though I have all faith, so that I could remove mountains, and have no charity, I am nothing. And though I bestow all my goods to feed the poor, and though I give my body to be burned, and have no charity, it profited me nothing. Charity suffered long, and is kind; charity envied not; charity vaunted, not itself, is not puffed up, doth not behave itself unseemly, seeker not her own, is not easily provoked, thinkers no evil; Rejoice not in iniquity, but rejoiced in the truth;" This could be the best magical part in the bible because within few lines it says how love is important and the importance of love you should feel yourself. I hope this chapter will add value to your life and have a right understanding of the importance of self-love.

THIRTEEN
EVERYBODY CAN BE HAPPY

This chapter is taken from my blog, which I felt useful when you become a changed man by finding the right path for your life.

Well, well, well, we all had our happiest moments as well as the saddest moments in our life. Some moments we often remember, others not. The point is in our life we all experience happiness and sadness. When we were children, we would always show fake sadness towards our parents to get the toy we want, for the chocolate we want, etc. When we grow up, our thinking changes, our need changes. In our teenage, we might show sad faces to get different things, surely not for a toy. In our adulthood the commitment changes, requirement changes so do the expressions of sadness also changes. If we look into our life a little deep, what could see us? We could see a few things there. Firstly, our life is filled with emotions. There is not even a single second void, if there is no happiness there will be sadness and vice versa. Secondly, we often search for happiness because we are sad, not because we want happiness. For example, if you have a massive debt obviously you will be tense and sad if things are not going in the way you thought, and here, before you had the massive debt you might have happiness, but how much did you enjoy it? How much do you value that time? Did you even know you had happiness in your life that time? Most of the people don't. Only when you are sad, you will start to search for the most important thing in your life, that is happiness. Whatever the job we do, people we met, or whatever the things we do in our life is to stay happy and if possible, make others also happy, but the problem is we only search for happiness if we are sad. I personally did not understand why it is like that? We buy new clothes just because we want them not because we need them, we buy a new phone just to replace the old ones but for getting happiness, we need to become sad first and that is wrong. Third, our attitude, most of us have an attitude that happiness is something that should be gifted by someone else, or sometimes we may have a thought like this unless and until a particular thing is done, I won't be happy. Fundamentally, that sort of attitude will not bring happiness to anyone's life. So, happiness is not a gift, happiness is not something we should look at only when we are sad. Then what is happiness? Before answering that question, we should understand one thing about pain. Pain is something that is very complex and constant. If we took a scale of 1 to 10 almost everyone will put 5 or 7 but the circumstances and situations vary at large. The situation I find painful may not be as painful for you, and vice-versa. So, pain plays an important role in our happiness. Now coming back to our question, what is happiness? Happiness is life. According to what I have learned, happiness is synonymous with life. Happiness is the reason why we all have life. How to live that life? It is not by searching for it, instead of by controlling and suppressing and handling our pain effectively.

If you are not sure how to be happy all the time, you may start doing a few basic things. As I always say, reading books doesn't matter it's fiction or non-fiction, whatever, just read. It will open up new perceptions that will help you to live a good life and help you counter your pain. You should treat pain as clothes if you are not required also, you should grab it. Things should not control your happiness, traffic block should not control your happiness, your happiness has only one control your life. From the world's richest person to the poorest one has seen problems but being sad because if it is neither a solution nor excuse so, keep your life within your life and make it happy forever. Help others and make them happy as well, as we are aware of positive attracts positive. Take out your fear from your body and soul through scientific prayers. Happiness will come to you gradually. Being happy is the best medicine, for all diseases, being happy is the doorway to all successes. You will not become happy after becoming successful; you will become successful when you are happy. If you are sad all the time, how will you use the tools available at your deposition for success, you will be crib cry about everything. So, being happy in life, if you are alive, you should be happy other circumstances are inevitable. You may do mental exercises, physical exercises to keep yourself clean internally. The most important thing is you should do what you love to do but in order to do you should understand that happiness is life not the effect of the result of your activities, circumstances, and situations.

In conclusion, everyone can be happy irrespective of our physical state and surroundings but what we don't understand is apart from the biological meaning of life, life is also called happiness. It is not a state or emotion, it is you.

FOURTEEN

SEARCH THEORY

This chapter is very important for those who feel their life stagnant even after understanding the idea behind finding the right path. This one is taken from my blog.

We are living in the world of success, lots of people always talk about success, I love to explore the possibilities and different meanings of human life success. We have seen people become legends, we have seen revolutionists, game-changers, inspirational stories of everything, every day. Furthermore, we know the opportunities presented by life, the number of choices we have, etc. we have read so many books, articles, we have seen so many YouTube videos, etc. about it. We know what is life. We are ambitious, we have targets, goals and most of us work really hard to get our respective goals. But still, sometimes we fail, we regret, we lose. We move away from the goal, sometimes we forget what we are doing, why we are doing it? Sometimes we felt life has no meaning, feels like life is not moving. We might feel depressed, these things happen in life.

The question is, do you ever wonder why this is happening? Why is this all sort of chaos? Why? Why? Why? The answer is not complicated, we will understand once we finish reading this article.

To find the answer first, we will check what is the basic requirement for a successful life or simply a happy life. I hope you already know the answer and that is hope, love, determination, goal, positive attitude, healthy subconscious mind, etc. we know this stuff but even though we have all these things we followed the right path we might feel the same stagnant effect in life. Felt like nothing is achieved. Nothing great happened. When we think of something, all we can see are problems without any solution. Even though we are self-aware, motivated and learning, in our life we feel so small and life is stuck. The concern is not with love, hope, or any other stuff of life. The concern is we are missing a small thing, a small process, and that process is search.

You may wonder what the hell is this guy talking about. I'm talking simple, naked truth here. Search is the element we miss in our life. Any failure, any chaos, any trouble in life is happening because we are not giving importance to search. No book or video will tell you the importance of search in life. Searching is the process that glues all other processes together. The love, care, passion, healthy subconscious mind, everything is of no use if you are not searching or not fall in love with the process of searching. If you have a habit of searching, your life will not be stagnant because it is common sense that for searching for something we need to move. When you define your life or goals it must possess the door for search otherwise you either end up in failure or you give up and deviate from what you want.

Let's take an example to understand further, consider you wanted to start something, and you started with your idea with your knowledge, you may flourish or perish initially but the thing you started is already stagnant because idea and knowledge are not getting updated or upgraded. Eventually, if you are not upgrading it will collapse, and how you will upgrade? You will only upgrade if you have the mentality for searching for things. Every successful people keep on searching, they set the goal and love the process of searching. Life will be awesome if you have the attitude of search.

The question is what should a person search? I would say anything. Because in order to live your life, you don't need any reason. You have a life that you got, not because of your ability or your achievements. Everything comes after you got a life, so, what we can do with our life is we can evolve ourselves. How we can evolve? Evolution through searching. When you search, you learn, and learning is fun. Search for love, search for care, do some kind of searches. Let's say you want love, and you're sitting simply hoping love will come to you, then it will not happen. Start searching for it, then only you will get it. The love you will receive may be unique to you, but you will only know when you start searching for it.

In conclusion, the searching mentality is the key to all kinds of success. The success for you may not be the one you think, but if you want to know, you have to start searching for it. Remember, the glue of all elements for a successful life is a searching attitude. Fall in love with the process of search, your life will be happy. The process of search is what defines you, not the goal. For example, a drug lord can become the world's richest man so do a legit businessman, which field you improvise in your search defines you. Anyway search and live life to its fullest.

FIFTEEN

THE CHANGED MAN

Once you follow the steps, understand how simple life is, once you started to get the satisfaction that you were searching for, for a long time, once you started traveling through the new path you are a changed man. You have to leave all that happened in the past, I mean those that pulled you down for a long time. You should value the change that occurred in the course of life. If you are able to figure out the path that you wanted to travel then you did something extra that an ordinary man never did that you are an extraordinary man right now. You will become an inspiration to at least your family, you are now motivation to the people younger than you, you are not an ordinary man anymore. It is a new beginning in your life, it is the moment you will feel at most satisfaction, irrespective of the results. If you ask me, is there no more challenges after becoming a changed man? I would say no, there will be lot more challenges, but the point is you are facing with much more confidence, and more important you are facing it with the right experience. Also, you should not get blind by your achievements. Your life is now a testimony for faith, belief, and dreams. Respect it, protect it, and love it.

In the long run, you will have to give all the knowledge to the needy who actually dream to become something. I don't have to tell you the qualities of a changed man, you already know it once you follow the right path. Now a man has changed himself for the greater good and his life will be a testimony always, forever.

SIXTEEN

RITUALS AND RECIPES

This chapter is all about some tips that might help you in situations. I called them recipes and also there are certain must-do things that will help you move up in your life. I called them rituals.

The recipes are:

When you are struggling with a problem

When you are struggling to find a solution to your problem, imagine you are taking the problem, putting it into a toilet, and flushing it. If it is not gone, flush twice. Now it is gone, feel that peace in mind. By doing it repeatedly, a solution will reveal to you.

How to cool off

People used to say that when you are angry, you should count one to ten to cool off. Practically, it won't work because we are already in a different mode, and we won't be able to think about counting numbers and all. But you can do a counting exercise for two to five minutes, before you go to bed or after you wake up or whenever it is free time for you. Do this repeatedly, you will be able to control your anger eventually.

When to give positive suggestions

You may hear that the best time to suggest positive notes to the brain is at the time just after waking up in the morning or before sleep at night. It won't work if you are tensed or worried or if you got up abruptly. It will only work whenever you go to bed or wake up with a calm and peaceful mind.

What to do when you are sad?

So sad at the moment, then stand up, take a deep breath, close your eyes, and then walk as long as you can in a straight line, immediately your concentration shift from sadness to target and that will erase the sadness.

How to create concentration?

Try to create an image of something you like in your mind in a calm state that will improve your concentration. Remember, you must create it from scratch, not just show it.

How to start creating habits?

Wanted to do something, but unable to do it, then do this: First, forget about your brain for a moment, stop listening to it. Once you wake up, take a piece of paper and write down what you want to do and how you want to do it, whenever you are unable to do take out the book to read, and do it. Continue the process until it becomes natural to you.

How do get sleep?

Unable to sleep do this: First put your phone on DND, now sit slightly slanted in a chair, close your eyes, and now say sleep, sleep, sleep in your mind in a very calm, tempting, smooth voice. You will fall asleep within 3-5 minutes. Continue till your brain adapt to sleep naturally.

When to pray?

Set up a "Prayer clock" to get maximum juice in a day! Here's how to do it? Divide your day into small-time capsules. E.g.: - 2hrs, therefore, 12-time capsules, pray at the beginning and end of each capsule or a collection of capsules. The prayer can be spiritual, religious, or scientific but, in each capsule certain tasks must be completed, beginning prayer should be what you need, ending prayer for showing gratitude, if you practice this you will be able to achieve time management, effective scheduling, strong belief system, faith, concentration, peace, eventually a level of happiness and freedom.

How to change habits?

Wanted to change any habit? First, you need to find out what you do instead of your current habit because the habit cannot be stopped. We can only change it to something else. So, the first step finds out what you are going to do instead, otherwise, it is a waste of time.

There are so many other tips that might come in handy along with this that I publish in my social media also you may follow on yourquote.in/ebyalex Rituals are some must-do things such as

- A cold shower everyday morning would be good

- Reading books every day again morning is the best time.

- Physical and mental exercises are important.

- Work schedule and timetable should be made and stick to it

- Pray daily meditate

- Learn something new related to your goal daily.

- Do not be afraid or worried, life will move on as always.

- Be positive and keep all negativity away.

- There are a few suggestions of the book may look into:

- Power of subconscious mind by Joseph Murphy

- Think and grow rich by Napoleon Hill

- Atomic habits by James clear

- Corporate Chanakya by Radhakrishnan Pillai

- The subtle art of not giving a f**k by Mark Manson

There are a lot of other books as well but as we are going to find out the path these books will definitely help.

Process

Pictorial representation of process;

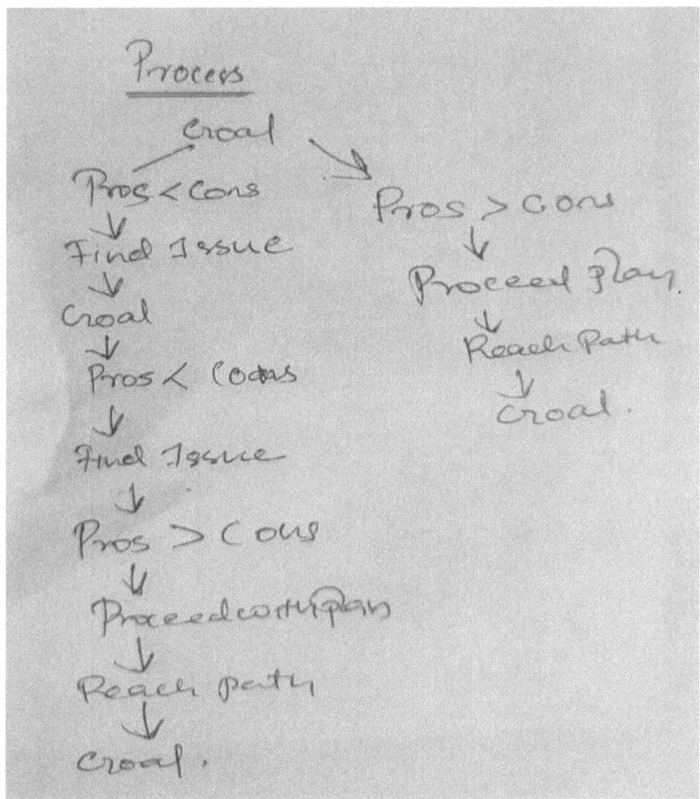

Path choosing method

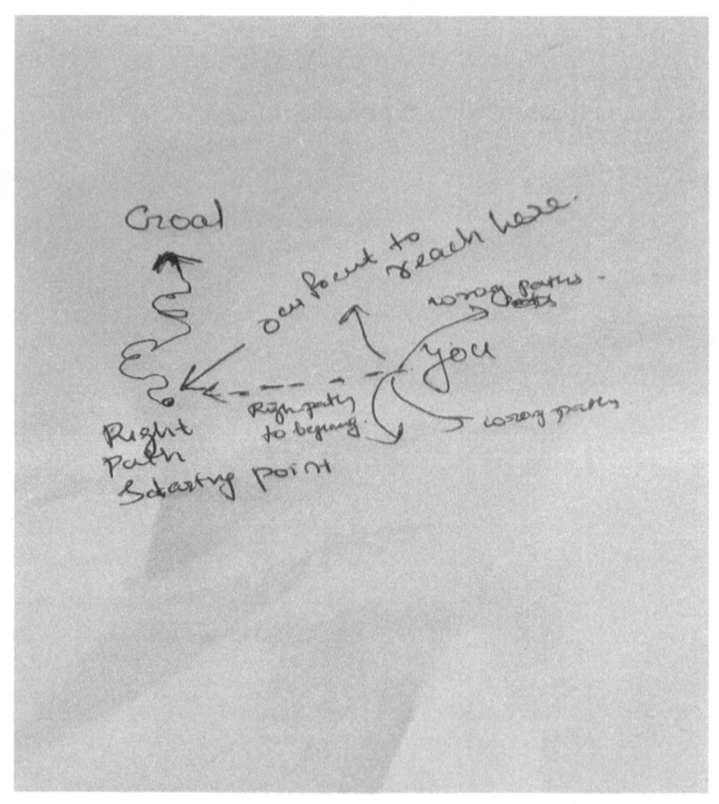

Process flow

www.ingramcontent.com/pod-product-compliance
Lightning Source LLC
Chambersburg PA
CBHW031401160726
47993CB00003B/1067